W9-AQL-848

PORTFOLIO F

METROPOLITAN SEMINARS IN ART

Great Periods in Painting

PORTFOLIO F
The World Triumphant: THE BAROQUE

BY JOHN CANADAY

ART EDITOR AND CRITIC
THE NEW YORK TIMES

THE METROPOLITAN MUSEUM OF ART

© 1959 by The Metropolitan Museum of Art

Printed in U. S. A.

ND
1135
.M5x
v. 6

THE WORLD TRIUMPHANT

The Baroque

AS THE great centuries of art recede in time, we see them in less and less detail. Ancient Greece, emerging from an unrecorded past, reaching its climax in the Golden Age, and declining as its world was absorbed by Rome, seems all of a piece. The Middle Ages are unified around a core of miracle and mystery, which gives a dominant character to an art that is full of contradictions and diversity when seen at the searching range of the scholar. In the Renaissance, closer to us in time and in ways of thought, we see more variety. And when we consider the seventeenth century, the impression of variety increases.

It was an age that demanded painting at every turn and offered the artist a wider scope than ever before. The number and kinds of patrons increased. The irreparable split of the Church into its Catholic and Protestant branches gave a new philosophical diversity to Christian art. The growth of states brought with it a new consciousness of art as a national expression. Monarchs attached painters to their retinues in increasing numbers and for new reasons—including, in France, propagandistic ones (if a word with unpleasant associations may be used to describe art of a high level dedicated to the glorification of a regime). Churches and public buildings rose in abundance, with vaults to be covered with painting and walls to be lined with pictures. Palaces grew in size, to such a degree that earlier ones like the Medici villa and the Gonzaga palace were modest and intimate by

comparison. And a new class of patrons appeared, the prosperous burghers, the practical men of commerce, who were not interested in esthetics but who did enjoy owning pictures and expected their tastes to be served, thus giving impetus to the exploration of new subjects or to fresh ways of treating old ones. The cozy houses of the burghers were filled with portraits of the owners and their families, pictures of the objects and the landscapes they loved, and scenes of daily life that were more interesting to these good people than religious dramas or intellectual speculations.

Yet in spite of its diversity the art of the seventeenth century does have a unifying characteristic. We have called this portfolio "The World Triumphant" because the century was, in spite of all exceptions and all variations on the theme, a worldly one. The word should not be taken with its derogatory associations but rather as meaning "of or pertaining to the world" and man's direct experience in it.

Mannerism to Baroque: El Greco

El Greco's *Adoration of the Shepherds* (Plate F1) hardly bears us out; it is anything but worldly. But a glance at El Greco's dates, 1541 to 1614, shows that we are only turning the corner into the new century, as we were about to do when we concluded our last discussion with Tintoretto's *Baptism of Christ* (Plate

5

60926

Figure 1

E12). The flickering lights, the pungent darks, and the elongation of swelling, contracting, and twisting forms in both pictures are evidence that Tintoretto was El Greco's master, at least by example, although most early histories refer to both painters as disciples of Titian. It is thought, also, that El Greco saw Michelangelo's work when he stayed in Rome.

El Greco, as this nickname indicates, was a Greek (his real name was Domenicos Theotocopoulos) who, when he was about twenty-five, went to Venice. By 1577, however, he was established in Toledo, the center of traditional Spanish Catholicism, with its odd combination of aristocracy and mysticism, austerity and hysteria. Here the religious spirit of seventeenth-century Spain was manifest in all its intensity and near-morbidity, sometimes in forms of the most forbidding severity, sometimes in eruptions of emotional excess. As if he had been searching for his spiritual land and had found it at last, El Greco remained in Toledo for the rest of his life. The court had moved to Madrid, and Toledo, on a rocky height bordered by precipitous gorges, must already have had the character of isolation within a spiritual tradition that one still feels there.

We do not know a great deal about El Greco as a man. His contemporaries have left stories of mild eccentricities. Speaking to a fellow painter in Rome, he made references to his "inner light," but one wonders whether the emphasis placed on these isolated bits of information is inspired as much by the man as by his painting, which on the face of it is shaped by wild visionary fervor. El Greco's style is at least as intellectual in its conception as it is emotional in its end effect. Perhaps the ultimate summary of Spanish mysticism had to be made by an outsider—this Greek who came by way of Italy—who combined objectivity with inborn sympathy. Even at its most intense, El Greco's art has none of the irrational quality of visionary hysteria. No hysteric, not even an "inspired" one, created the intricate and beautifully calculated forms of *The Adoration of the Shepherds*. They knot and twist, soar and descend, emerge and recede, move and pause, with a perfection beyond accident, an expressiveness beyond mere impulse. They have the assurance that comes from technical mastery built upon study, contemplation, and a continued effort from picture to picture to develop forms appropriate to an expression. That "inspiration" may account for an occasional great picture when impulse and a certain amount of lucky chance fall into happy juxtaposition is conceivable; that a series of masterpieces over a long life-

time could be so produced is an absurd idea. *Saint John's Vision of the Mysteries of the Apocalypse* (*Figure 1*) is anguished in its intensity, but it is not the product of a creative paroxysm. Its extreme distortions, its flickering and wavering surface, like a pattern of cold flames, the sudden shifts in perspective that account for so much of its supernatural character—all these have their counterparts, in milder form, in El Greco's earlier work.

El Greco, isolated in his emphatic individuality, is at the same time cousin or forebear to half a dozen schools or movements. Trained in Greece in the tradition of Byzantine icon painting, he has been called its climax in a European translation. He is often considered a mannerist, in the extensions of that term beyond its immediate Italian origins. And twentieth-century expressionists have claimed him as their ancestor in free distortion of form and color, at whatever violation of natural appearances, for the liberation of expressive im-

Alinari   *Figure 2*

7

Alinari

Figure 3

pulse. All these connections are legitimate enough and should be obvious. But El Greco is also called a precursor of baroque art, the art of the seventeenth century. This takes more explaining and requires first an examination of some typical examples of baroque style.

Baroque and the Counter Reformation

"Baroque" is an elusive word, easy to define in any one of its several meanings but difficult to pin down in its multiple overlapping and contradictory uses. As a strictly defined word it is still in the process of crystallization. In the meantime it means one thing in one context and others elsewhere. It is freely used in ways dictionaries do not sanction, and some dictionary definitions are in opposition to the ideas of contemporary critics who have been re-evaluating baroque art for several decades.

Most people think of "baroque" as designating an elaborate and irregular anticlassical style of seventeenth-century ecclesiastical architecture, full of broken and twisting forms (*Figure 2*), and the painting and sculpture corollary to this architecture. Yet it may refer equally to severely classical architecture and to certain painting in the classical tradition, as we shall see. It may refer without restriction to the seventeenth century as a whole, and it is sometimes used as a general term indicating eccentric or fanciful modes of painting, architecture, dress, or behavior in any period. At least one dictionary still refers to "bad taste" in a definition of this protean word, a hang-over from a generation of critics whose blanket rejection of baroque as an unseemly lapse in the history of the creative arts sprang from an exaggerated reverence for simplicity and "purity."

In view of these confusions, we might best begin with an example of baroque art from the later period, one that is undeniably baroque by a majority of definitions, the ceiling of the church of Saint Ignatius in Rome. It was painted by Andrea Pozzo (1642–1709), an artist who was a member of the Jesuit order; his ceiling is a tribute to the principles of its founder, Ignatius Loyola.

The Glorification of the Company of Jesus (*Figure 3*), as the ceiling is called, covers the entire vault of the nave. By a tour de force of perspective design we appear to be looking upward through an impressive architectural con-

Alinari

Figure 4

struction (itself an excellent example of baroque style, by the way) that tops the actual walls of the church. It continues them so convincingly that it is difficult, and sometimes impossible, to tell exactly where the real architecture ends and the painted forms begin. These elaborate columns, shafts, moldings, arches, pedestals, and a hundred other architectural representations lead us into the expanse of heaven, past armies of figures that fly, cling, tumble, leap, and gesture grandiloquently toward the focal point of the Holy Trinity, to which every element of the design

9

is directed. Light radiates from this center, illuminating the objects near it and shedding some of its glow onto the lower figures, which are painted to give the illusion of receiving illumination also from the real windows of the church and the painted openings of the perspective architecture. We have called this painting a tour de force; the term may seem inadequate to describe a staggering triumph of perspective and chiaroscuro techniques, but it is apt if it implies that the breathtaking illusion is the result of skillful manipulation rather than great creative power.

Toward what end is this illusion directed? The theme of the picture (the ceiling is in fact a gargantuan picture painted on a continuous surface) refers to the function of the Jesuit order, which was to spread the gospel throughout the world, not by inspirational evangelism but by reasonable persuasion through study and teaching. The four quarters of the globe are represented symbolically, although it is not easy to connect the group symbolizing America (*Figure 4*) with the early days of the New World. Pozzo left a notation explaining the figures in his composition, but the allegory is swallowed up by the exciting illusion of tumultuous forms in tumultuous space disciplined by an organizational scheme of false architecture in true perspective.

The illusion is so complete that the vault, in effect, disappears. One can find no indication in the illustration that the ceiling is a half-round, or barrel, vault. An observer who stands within the church is at almost as great a loss to decipher the vault's curve. He must concentrate, must pit his own perception against the illusion, or he loses consciousness of the ceiling. Of course he is supposed to lose consciousness of it; in this way the illusion becomes symbolical: the physical limitations of matter (the solidity of the ceiling) have been defeated, overcome, eradicated, by a spiritual scheme.

In an even more direct way the ceiling is the pictorial equivalent of the *Spiritual Exercises* of Ignatius Loyola, whose church this is. The *Spiritual Exercises* is a series of arguments that take the reader step by logical step toward the point where, finally, the supernatural becomes real. Just so, in the ceiling, we believe as we move upward from the actual walls of the church and imperceptibly enter the painted scheme on the vault. We continue to believe as we are led from detail to detail, for each is credible upon the acceptance of the preceding one. Irrevocably, then, we must accept the final revelation of the Holy Trinity, toward which each detail leads us.

On the floor of the church there is a marble marker specifying the point at which the observer should stand to receive the illusion in its perfection. By standing there he willingly subjects himself to a point of view, just as in accepting the doctrines of the Church he willingly enters a scheme whose intricacies are made meaningful to him by the chosen instruments of the Church—in this case, of course, the teachings of the Jesuits.

However, let us look more questioningly at this ceiling and the means by which it achieves its end. By another interpretation, the "spiritual" scheme is created in such tangible terms that its effect is not to elevate the spirit but to stagger and overpower the senses. It appeals first through worldly experience of the grandiose, the spectacular, and the physically impressive, rather than through mystical revelation.

Baroque art was an instrument of the Counter Reformation, through which the Church sought to maintain or regain its influence by appealing to the kind of experience people understand most easily. Experience hits most directly, though not always most deeply, through the senses, through sensations of pleasure and pain that leave indelible impressions on us as we live in the physical world. Baroque artists frequently capitalized on the immediacy of these emotional reactions, and a "spiritual" art became an art of sensation.

The legitimacy of playing upon sensation as

a back door to the spirit could be debated endlessly. Sensation was, nevertheless, basic in the religious art of the Counter Reformation. Sometimes it overemphasized painful experiences represented with unqualified realism; sometimes it employed intellectual detachment. *The Martyrdom of Saint Bartholomew* (*Figure 5*) by Jusepe Ribera (1591–1652), a Spaniard who later worked in Italy where he developed a somewhat more gracious style, is a standard example of objective representation of an anguishing subject, an approach that suited an age that responded to the idea of torture endured for faith. But the extreme example of physical sensation as an assault on the sensibilities of the spirit is the celebrated sculpture, *The Ecstasy of Saint Theresa* (*Figure 6*), by Gian Lorenzo Bernini (1598–1680).

The swooning emotionalism of this remarkable work made it a popular favorite for generations, precisely because its recall of physical sensations is potent, even when its nature is not recognized by the observer. Stripped of its spiritual veneer, the hyperemotionalism would be downright embarrassing. The statue is a specific instance of the "bad taste" attributed to baroque art by a generation of critics who also objected to its complicated realism. But *The Ecstasy of Saint Theresa* is admired as a pure example of several legitimate baroque principles. The wildly emotional effect is created shrewdly, cannily, with infinite aplomb. The artist remains so coolly outside the emotional extreme of the subject that the statue exemplifies the consummate calculation and absolute technical mastery upon which the most impressive baroque art is based. (The design and construction of some baroque edifices that seem the result of pure fantasy was made possible only by the application of mathematical theories new to the century.)

Sculptors are still likely to deny *The Ecstasy of Saint Theresa* any merit, insisting that the point of departure of sculpture must be its material: stone sculpture must express the stone; wood or metal sculpture must be as woody or as metallic as possible. But *The Ecstasy of Saint Theresa* denies this principle in every detail. Its tons of marble, in the first place, seem to be released from the power of gravity to float in air. And the marble is transformed into dimpled flesh, soft curls, fluttering draperies of different textures (*Figure 7*), and even, as an ultimate denial of the stone, into vaporous clouds. But here, too, the group is typically baroque. The textural illusions, the shimmering light and shadow that dapple the forms, apply the principles of painting to the medium of carving. In baroque various arts are fused: sculpture may imitate painting; painting may imitate sculpture and architecture, as in Pozzo's ceiling. A façade may be conceived less as a structure than as a mass of sculpture, or planned in terms of the flickering light and shifting forms more natural to painting. No boundaries are recognized between the arts and their materials, or they are so fused that the transitions become imperceptible. It is worth noticing that it was in the seventeenth century that opera came into its own—opera, the "impure" art, a synthesis of literary drama, music in a variety of forms,

Anderson

Figure 5

11

Alinari

Figure 6

and visual arts. There are purists who do not accept opera as an art form and purists who do not accept Bernini, but by another standard, baroque "bad taste" is part of a complicated harmony. Its flagrant violations of purist standards are not arbitrary, willful, or capricious but part of a logical process.

We began this introduction to one aspect of baroque art with El Greco as a possible prototype. It is time now for us to see whether the possibility holds. In several ways it does. Most obviously, El Greco's winding, upward-moving patterns have at least a coincidental echo in Pozzo's ceiling. His intensity may come close to agony, a factor that has led writers to compare his twisted, elongated figures to bodies tortured on the rack. But the division between El Greco and the baroque examples we have seen could be much narrower than it is and still be the sharpest kind of separation. For El Greco is visionary and unrealistic, making his effect through the abstractions of shapes and color; Pozzo, Ribera, and Bernini are realistic, making their effect through the actuality of their images. Pozzo's figures may fly, as real ones cannot, may hover in space, may perform impossible actions. Nevertheless they are literally presented. It is because they are so *real* that we are impressed by the spectacular stagecraft of the superproduction in which they are involved. El Greco speaks to us of inner miracles; Pozzo shows us physical ones. El Greco elevates the spirit; Pozzo performs feats of levitation. El Greco's figures are dematerialized—matter consumed by the inexplicable, while Pozzo's are materialized as a didactic explanation. El Greco, in short, is otherworldly, while Pozzo speaks in terms of this world even when his subject is mystery. His ceiling triumphantly declaims: this is not theory, spiritual fable, legend, or a vision. This is *so*, and may be accepted without question, just as the teachings of the Church are so in the minds of the faithful, and may be accepted without question, as surely as you are standing there and seeing this miracle take place in fact.

Anderson   *Figure 7*

Early Baroque Realism: Caravaggio

In beginning our discussion with *The Glorification of the Company of Jesus*, which was painted between 1691 and 1694, we have started at the end of the baroque century. The century was one of reaction against mannerism by a return to the grand manner of the High Renaissance, a reaction that had begun a hundred years before. For their importance as initiators of this movement we must set down the names of the Carracci, Lodovico (1555–1619) and his nephews Agostino (1557–1602) and Annibale (1560–1609), who developed eclectic styles and established an influential art school in Bologna in 1585. But the great revolutionary figure who opened the century was a younger man, Michelangelo Merisi da Caravaggio (1573–1610).

Caravaggio had a vast effect on European painting in his own century and he con-

13

Figure 8

tinued to influence painters, including Cézanne, quite directly through the nineteenth. In important ways he is a powerful force today on painters who seem in no way to resemble him. He was painting in Italy while El Greco, an aging man, was at work in Spain. And although El Greco lived four years beyond Caravaggio's early death, the younger man revolutionized painting to such a degree that a century might have separated them. In his comparative isolation El Greco found no disciples. Our own time has rediscovered him as the first "modern" painter, after the passage of three hundred years in which painting followed the direction set by Caravaggio.

Caravaggio was a rebel, one of the first painters to be subjected to the kind of criticism and opposition with which the revolutionary painters of our time are familiar and one of the first, too, to flaunt his scorn of tradition, as today's painters like to do. But Caravaggio's revolution was not directed toward intellectual abstraction, as the twentieth century's significant revolutions have been. It was in the opposite direction, toward acute realism. After some early works of great elegance connected with mannerism, like *The Musicians* (Portfolio 6, Plate 70), Caravaggio rejected mannerist intellectualism and high style and set about to bring painting into the realm of direct human experience. He was criticized because his saints were represented as ordinary people; he had to re-do his first important commission when the initial version was rejected because Saint Matthew was shown as a common man. But during his short life, full of brawling and arrests, Caravaggio found enough patrons sympathetic to his ideas to leave behind a handful of masterpieces in which human drama brings religious experience into the realm of worldly sensation. The reality of the miraculous, which we have seen expressed in the grand manner in Pozzo's theatrical allegory, was depicted in earthy terms by Caravaggio.

His *Conversion of Saint Paul* (Plate F 2) brings us into the presence of the event as it happens; its reality is all but tangible. Since this sounds as if *The Conversion of Saint Paul* and *The Glorification of the Company of Jesus* appeal to the observer in the same way, it is natural to ask why Caravaggio is a great painter while Pozzo is remembered as an expert workman. In part the difference is that Caravaggio was an innovator, which gives him historical significance. More important, however, is the difference between great drama and expert theater. The dramatic force of *The Conversion of Saint Paul* goes beneath the visual impact by which it makes its first appeal. *The Glorification of the Company of Jesus* makes a staggering first impression but loses power as we continue to study it, becoming a gigantic decorative novelty in the form of an allegorical diagram. Caravaggio's picture draws us further and further into a deepening experience. It might be argued that *The Conversion of Saint Paul* has the advantage of being seen at close range, for it occupies one wall of a small chapel. On the other hand, the Sistine Ceiling and Michelangelo's *Last Judgment* are evidence enough that huge scale need not mean a thinning out of force and strength.

It takes some effort to recognize the revolutionary character of Caravaggio's realism, since we have spoken of the "realism" of early renaissance painters absorbed in the study of the visible world and the means to represent it. But these early realists held always to an ideal concept; no matter how objective their studies of perspective, anatomy, plants, and all the other phenomena of the visual world, painters like Masaccio, Piero della Francesca, Mantegna, and Leonardo regarded nature as the raw material for the expression of an ideal beyond objective reality. They saw realism as an approach to the universal order, investigated the world as a place that might yield the secrets

by which some ultimate harmony could be attained, some meaning of life understood.

Caravaggio scoffed at such ideas. As an anti-idealist he insisted that nature alone was his master, his final one. For Caravaggio only the experience of the senses was legitimate material for art. All of this sounds as if he should have been a vulgar, heavy-handed, and thoroughly obvious painter—and so he appeared to many of his contemporaries, accustomed as they were to the eclectic idealism of Raphael's tradition or to the esthetic individuality of the mannerists.

But *The Conversion of Saint Paul* is certainly not vulgar, heavy-handed, or obvious. Its realistic components are dramatized, first of

Figure 9

15

Figure 10

all, by light. This is not the explosive light of Tintoretto, nor the wavering, inexplicable light of El Greco, but a strong, steady, brilliant, factual light that creates sharp edges, throws details into relief, and convincingly defines the solidity of mass and dramatizes its components. Caravaggio's realism is literal in proportion and in such detail as he includes. He paints the features of common people rather than idealized masks; he shows us draperies, flesh, pelts, and metal that are palpable in their veracity. But his artistry lies in the abstract factors that transform imitation into creation, and here nature is no longer Caravaggio's master.

He is a magnificent colorist; the commonest object takes on richness and consequence when he paints it. The realism of any part of his pictures is selective; the wrinkle in a face or the vein on a hand or a foot is introduced purposefully rather than as a random accident of na-

ture reproduced because it is present in the model. Apparent naturalness is subjected to brilliantly inventive compositional disciplines. If we could forget that the forms in Caravaggio's pictures are men, horses, and recognizable objects, if we could regard them only as volumes arranged in masterly balances and contrasts within the volume of space—if we could regard them as abstract forms, in other words—they would have their own excitement, their own monumentality, their own satisfying interrelationships apart from the stories they tell as the characters and properties of a drama. But Caravaggio's greatness as a realist lies in the fact that we cannot forget these characters and properties, that we are impressed with their indisputable existence.

The Tenebrists

All abstract considerations aside, Caravaggio's strong light and shadow was so startling, so effective, and seemed so easy to imitate that it produced followers on an international scale. Some reduced the Caravaggesque drama to a shallow formula; others turned his devices to their own expressive uses. In Spain and the Low Countries especially these "tenebrists," or shadow painters, flourished. We have already seen the Spaniard Ribera, and the reader may want to make his own comparison of Ribera's *Martyrdom of Saint Bartholomew* with Caravaggio's *Conversion of Saint Paul*.

One of the most interesting of the tenebrists was a Frenchman, Georges de La Tour (1593–1652), who, after having been lost for many generations, has been rediscovered in this century, a new old master. La Tour seems not to have been a very conspicuous painter during his lifetime. As centuries passed he became little more than a name. His paintings were attributed to various other artists, French, Italian, Spanish, and Dutch, who worked in the tradition of Caravaggio. The rediscovery of La Tour began slowly in 1863 during researches in the archives of Nancy, the ancient capital of his native Lorraine, but another half century passed before it proceeded in earnest. His paintings have now been recollected around his name, and he is probably better known today than he was in his lifetime. Records show that he reached the status of a painter to the king, but most of his work was done for the duke of Lorraine—an important but provincial patron in a country where the brilliance of Paris reduced all else to obscurity.

When Lorraine was attacked by the plague in 1631, La Tour painted several episodes from the story of Saint Sebastian to invoke the saint's protection for the duke and other patrons. *Saint Sebastian Found by Saint Irene* (Plate F 3) and *The Conversion of Saint Paul* show how individual two pictures may be in spirit, through the stylistic devices are similar.

La Tour's flavor is rather dry, his restraint so extreme that even a subject of anguish or sorrow becomes one of reverie. He often forced light and shadow to their limits by painting nighttime subjects illuminated by a single candle. But the expressive intensities, which we might expect to find correspondingly heightened, are on the contrary chastened to peacefulness and a simplicity approaching naïveté. Their archaic rigidity make La Tour's figures seem foreign to their time, not by their quiet dignity but by their simple reverence.

Optical Truth: Velazquez

In spite of the exaggerations, artificialities, or disciplines that modify them, the paintings and sculpture we have been seeing (except, of course, El Greco's) take the visible world as a point of departure. The purest exemplar of visual realism in the seventeenth century, or virtually any other time, was Diego Rodríguez de Silva y Velazquez (1599–1660), who came as close as any painter has come, while remaining an artist, to re-creating literal, visual truth in paint. "Truth, not painting" was his own statement of the ideal he hoped to achieve.

The realism of Velazquez differs from that of Caravaggio—and of every other painter before him—in one fundamental way. Caravaggio turned to the world and represented it without the artificialities by which the mannerists transformed it. But Velazquez turned to visible reality and studied it as an optical phenomenon. He tried to reproduce exactly what his eye saw—and no more.

His famous *Venus and Cupid* (*Figure 8*) shows the goddess as a lovely girl, completely unidealized, which is in line with Caravaggio's

Anderson

Figure 11

17

Figure 12

Caravaggio's standards, it means an incomplete rendering of their form. This is optical truth—true to what the eye actually perceives under a given set of circumstances rather than true to what actually exists. It is a principle that we will see pushed to further conclusions two centuries later by the impressionists in France. Another Spaniard, Francisco Goya, was to say, "I want to train my brush not to see more than I do," a statement that could have come from Velazquez.

We have seen Velazquez's most complicated picture based on these principles, *The Maids of Honor* (Portfolio 2, Plate 19). In the majority of his pictures Velazquez obviously had to synthesize the whole from many parts, since the whole could not be set up all at once for him to paint. This was the case in the equestrian portrait, *Don Gaspar de Guzmán, Count Duke of Olivares* (Plate F4). The head and probably the general outlines of the figure would have been done from life. A clothed dummy might replace the model thereafter, and the handsome landscape was invented from observation of nature. The rearing horse had to be pieced together and, above all, the various elements of the picture had to be unified by knowledge of the action of light on material objects.

As an example of "optical truth" the picture is utterly convincing, but to an exceptional degree it has an additional appeal that is present in all of Velazquez's work: it is beautiful, all subject matter and all reflection of reality aside. As painting, as pure color, as pure manipulation of paint, it is beautiful. "Truth, not painting" is not an accurate description of Velazquez's art, although it is his own. If he had achieved nothing but the re-creation of optical truth he would, of course, have been not an artist but only a human lens, a mechanical eye. "Truth *through* painting" is a more accurate description of this art in which the image is created by films, layers, strokes, and gobbets of pigment that have made Velazquez the delight and the envy of pure painters ever since his time.

way of representing saints as ordinary beings. But in addition Velazquez has studied his model as a problem in the laws of vision. Where his eye cannot perceive detail, he does not paint detail; if his eye cannot distinctly see the line separating one fold of drapery from another, he does not paint it distinctly, whereas Caravaggio would have painted it as sharply as if he were seeing it at close range. The extreme example in *Venus and Cupid* is the reflection of the face of Venus in the mirror. Individual features are blurred because the mirror clouds them but also because from the distance at which he painted, Velazquez could perceive less in the mirror than could his model, at close range. And the bits of ribbon that fall over the mirror frame are reduced to areas of color and light, even though, by

Zurbarán and Murillo

Both Caravaggio and Velazquez are realists, but realists who discipline their vision according to the end in view, Caravaggio toward the organization of dramatic expression, Velazquez toward serene and noncommittal objectivity. Velazquez's friend and immediate contemporary, Francisco de Zurbarán (1598–1664), who was born within a year of Velazquez and died four years after him, painted with some of the same removed serenity but, much more than Velazquez, he regarded his subjects as problems in pure form.

Zurbarán has been increasingly appreciated in the wake of our understanding of other painters who at first seem to have little connection with him—even the cubists, whose studies in form begin with the geometrical premise that lies just beneath Zurbarán's surface. His *Saint Margaret* (*Figure 9*) is certainly more sculpturesque, by contemporary standards, than Bernini's sculpture *The Ecstasy of Saint Theresa*. The massed and simplified forms are represented compactly, without the softening play of intervening atmosphere with which Velazquez would have diffused them. Zurbarán should be recognized as a painter close to Caravaggio; other examples of his work would place him even more definitely in

the tenebrist group. Like Caravaggio he eliminates incidental detail, largely for purposes of design, whereas Velazquez would have eliminated, or only suggested them, for the purposes of his "truth." Zurbarán's truth is different. His art suggests the truth of thought arrived at by contemplation, the truth of ideas rather than of the eye's retina.

One more Spaniard, before we go north, represents another variant on baroque realism. The appealing sentimentality of Bartolomé Esteban Murillo (1618–1682) is in opposition to the objectivity of Velazquez and the austerity of Zurbarán. Out of critical favor just now, when "sentimental" is the most damning of adjectives, Murillo nevertheless is an admirable painter who has suffered from the extreme popularity of his worst pictures, representing cute urchins and almost mawkish madonnas. His *Saint Thomas of Villanueva Dividing His Clothing among Beggar Boys* (*Figure 10*), showing the saint as a child, afforded Murillo a perfect subject, simultaneously sentimental, religious, and genre. In this union of an artist's natural bent and a subject of wide appeal, Murillo painted at the top of his form. He is most closely associated with the subject of the Immaculate Conception (*Figure 11*), which he repeated many times. We may balk at the cloying sweetness and suspect the

Figure 13

19

repetition of the subject—it amounted to a kind of sinecure for him—but we must respect the staying power of these pictures, which have appealed so steadily to so many people over so many years, centuries that have seen art, life, and thought given many new directions.

Baroque in the North: Rubens

Between the art of the northern countries and the art of Italy, as we have seen them up to this century, there has been an important difference. The northern painters were interested in detailed, sometimes almost microscopic, reproduction of everything the eye could see. (As examples we note the Van Eycks, Robert Campin with his *Annunciation*, Hugo van der Goes with his *Adoration of the Shepherds*, which, in spite of its relatively large size, is in many ways a fabulous piece of miniature

Alinari

Figure 14

painting, and even Dürer and Holbein.) The Italians were interested in broader forms and more idealized standards of beauty, painted on the grand scale. (Giotto, Masaccio, Piero della Francesca, Raphael, and Michelangelo are examples.)

We saw the traditions produce a hybrid in the sixteenth-century art sponsored by Francis I at Fontainebleau. Now, in the seventeenth century, with more travel and other communication between the two sides of the Alps, we find these dividing lines tending to disappear, but a new kind of division, the split of the Church into Catholic and Protestant branches, created new contrasts.

The division was most pronounced in the tiny area of the Low Countries, with Flanders (Belgium) remaining Catholic and its neighbor Holland flourishing as a powerful Protestant center. The Fleming Rubens and the Dutchman Rembrandt, two artists whose names are pinnacles in art, represent the contrasting ways of thought of their century.

In a triumphant life Peter Paul Rubens (1577–1640) was a great painter, a diplomat, and an international figure. His good looks, intelligence, and vigorous normalness attracted the respect and affection of everyone from princes to servants. His personal life was as full and as rich as his paintings. Like Raphael before him he seems to have been a favorite of the gods; but more than Raphael's do, Rubens' paintings tell us of a human being whose appetite for life and physical capacity for enjoying it were so great that they might have overwhelmed a man without Rubens' understanding and power of organization.

Rubens is the perfect amalgam of northern realism and Italian grand idealism. In his early twenties he went to Rome. During these Italian years he traveled widely, met Italian painters, and listened to their discussions. Rubens observed the revival of the grand manner along the lines of the Carracci's school and studied the works of Raphael and Michelangelo that had inspired it. He saw Caravaggio's realistic

Figure 15

works and was sympathetic to them, or at least to their dramatic quality. When he returned to Flanders at the age of thirty-one, he combined fullness, turbulence, grand scale, and interest in mythological subjects on one hand and emotionalized religious ones on the other, with the traditional Flemish passion for the representation of the things of this world in all their variety of texture and form. In *The Rape of the Daughters of Leucippus* (Plate F 5), a typical and magnificent Rubens, we may at first see only the reflection of Italian baroque style in the tempestuous movement and noble scale of the drama. But more than any Italian, Rubens is fascinated with the light that plays on satin and reveals its texture, with the gleam of metal, the sheen of cascading blond hair, and the texture of abundant flesh. Compared with Velazquez's Venus or with the nudes of Titian, Rubens' bodies have an actuality beyond the objectivity of the first or the voluptuous associations of the second. Flesh as Rubens paints it, with its moisture, its warmth, its very structure as a substance with blood coursing through it, is a paean to the ebullient

forces of life. Rubens is baroque in the opulence of his jewels, flesh, and fabrics but he is also a true inheritor of a Flemish tradition that served a different purpose. The contrasts and harmonies of textures in the Campin altarpiece (Portfolio B, *Figure 19*), as one example, are part of the celebration of the mystical story of the Virgin; in *The Rape of the Daughters of Leucippus* they glorify the wonderful richness of the world of sensuous experience. This picture, like virtually all that Rubens painted until near the end of his life, is a scene of triumph, of exuberance, of the glory of the physical world.

The picture is from Rubens' third period, after the early Roman one when his work followed closely the models he most admired—Michelangelo, Raphael, and the Venetians—and a period marked by almost Caravaggesque light and fluid, dynamic compositions. The triumphant air of the third period, in which he fully matures as an artist without eclectic echoes, could symbolize his own physical vitality and intellectual alertness and the ex-

Figure 16

21

Figure 17

citement of the position he had attained. He was sought after by every court in Europe; on one occasion he received an order for more than three hundred paintings from the court of Russia. In his fourth period vast cycles of paintings came from his studio—his factory, it has been called, in which a regiment of assistants executed his designs. For the information of his purchasers Rubens kept records of which parts of a picture were from his own hand. His favorite assistant was Anthony Van Dyck (1599–1641), who became best known when he went to England as court painter to Charles I and, in pictures like *Robert Rich* (*Figure 12*), established a tradition of virtuosity in aristocratic portraiture that has borne his mark ever since. And Rubens' "factory" included many other painters of reputation, specialists in their fields like Frans Snyders (1579–1657), whose paintings of animals, particularly in hunting scenes like *A Boar Hunt* (*Figure 13*), were much sought after.

The Flemish were fond of sumptuous ar-

rangements of animals, birds, and still life. *Peacocks* (Plate F6) by Melchior D'Hondecoeter (1636–1695) has its own kind of opulence and love of material luxury on a princely scale; in Rubens, these qualities are raised from a level of delight in the things of life to delight, supreme joy, in life itself.

The works of his last years continue his hymn to the gloriousness of life, but in a more intimate, gentle way. In picture after picture he shows us his delight in the loveliness of his young second wife and their children (*Figure 14*). The pictures are happy and fresh, but occasionally we can imagine in them, beneath the lovingly applied surface, a hint of poignance, as if an aging man recognizes, with full awareness of the good fortune that has been his, that the great adventure must end.

Rembrandt

Among the young northerners in Rome at the same time as Rubens was a Dutchman named Pieter Lastman (1583–1633) who came strongly under the influence of Caravaggio. Although he was a bit heavy-handed, Lastman was a respectable enough painter. His name would

Figure 18

Figure 19

Figure 20

fort but suspicious of any suggestion of excess or high living. The painter depended more on portraits than anything else for his living. The lively demand was largely negated by intense competition; painters were safest, therefore, when they maintained, as Rembrandt was un-

crop up much less frequently if he had not become an influential teacher, numbering among his pupils another Dutchman, the young Rembrandt Harmensz. van Ryn (1606–1669). Lastman introduced Rembrandt to the baroque drama of vivid light and mysterious shadow; the younger painter's skill in its manipulation produced, as an example of a conspicuous kind, "The Night Watch" (Portfolio 7, Plate 73). Thereafter, increasingly, Rembrandt's drama grew quieter and deeper as he began to explore the nature and the motivations of human personality. For this reason or another, Rembrandt, who painted more and more to please himself rather than his customer, lost interest in competitive painting and spent his mature life in poverty.

The princely commissions that brought wealth to Rubens did not exist in Holland. The pomp and heightened emotionalism of southern baroque painting were unacceptable to the reserved, practical society of Protestant Holland and to the life of its burghers, who were cautious, a little tight-fisted, fond of com-

willing to do, a conventional approach, creating a technically skillful but flatly objective representation of the subject. The great portraitist was Frans Hals (about 1580–1666), whose works in a tight technique (*Figure 15*) and in a dashing, freely brushed one (*Figure 16*) not only pleased his customers but, to the maximum possible with the objective approach, were perceptive characterizations. But even Hals led a precarious financial life and ended his days on what we would call "relief."

Nothing interested Rembrandt more than the human face, not as a set of features to be reproduced or even, as in Hals's best works, a revelation of individual personality but as a clue to the sources of all human feeling. Caravaggio's insistence on using common people as models was extended by Rembrandt in his probing of the human spirit, for he found it most richly and poignantly revealed not in stories of miraculous events but in the miracle of the human soul, of human consciousness enriched and developed by the course of life in a world filled with joys, defeats, and tragedies. Kings, saints, and the other exceptional beings of legend and history interested him less than the anonymous inhabitants of the ghetto. When he painted a "nobleman" or a "knight," like the one in *The Man with the Golden Helmet* (*Figure 17*), he placed the trappings of jewels and fine robes on homely bodies or around faces seamed or swollen or scarred by buffet-

Figure 21

ings. The gleaming cloths and glistening metals, nominally the signs of worldly rank, become instead the symbols of noble spirit.

For Rembrandt, biblical stories like *The Return of the Prodigal Son* (*Figure 18*) are not demonstrations of dogma or illustrations of miraculous legend or history; they are accounts of human beings involved in the confused search for themselves that all of us experience, subject to motivations that we cannot always recognize even when they affect us most strongly. The shadowed faces he paints are those of men and women who have learned

that suffering and misfortune must be accepted with the other experiences by which providence reveals to us the reasons for our existence. His own face served him again and again as a subject over the years, showing him first as a young and confident and prosperous man (*Figure 19*) then through the period of his personal sorrow to the days of his old age (*Figure 20*). He painted his own image not because he was enamored of its ill-proportioned and coarsening features but because it was a face in which he could ponder the question of man's nature.

Rembrandt's *Old Woman Cutting Her Nails* (Plate F 7) could be regarded by a certain standard as a genre subject, showing an ordinary human being engaged in an insignificant bit of a day's activities. By this standard it would still be enjoyable as a technical masterpiece but it would hardly warrant its large size and dramatic presentation; it would be a waste of the time and skill of a superb painter. Its greatness lies beyond the technique or subject.

The fall of golden light reveals an inconsequential old woman about whom we know nothing except what we may surmise from her dress and physical characteristics. But we need know only that we are in the presence of a spiritual wholeness that gives meaning to life because it reduces to unimportance the suffering and decay of the body. If we had seen this woman at some important moment, posed self-consciously in her best clothes, the implications of the picture would be limited by the restricting specialness of the circumstances. Climactic moments are important as landmarks; they may bring forth vividly special aspects of our natures. But our lives from day to day are filled with a thousand unspectacular actions; by choosing one of them Rembrandt brings us nearer to the old woman. Instead of showing us one event in a life, he shows us something closer to life itself.

More importantly, the triviality of the action generalizes rather than individualizes the old

24

Figure 22

woman. We are conscious of her not as an individual but as an image representing all human beings who have weathered the hazards, the chances, the apparent chaos of life and must continue to do so; who have reached somehow an understanding that there are mysteries that justify our existence. These are the mysteries that Rembrandt ponders. He does not offer us an answer in so many words —nor does he suggest that there is one, beyond his conviction that man is noble—noble if only because he examines the nature of life and finds it intolerable, or meaningless, except as sustained by the life of the spirit.

The Dutch Scene

Economic and social conditions in Holland placed the artist in the position most familiar to him today—that of a man who paints pictures and offers them for sale, rather than one who executes commissions under contract. As a result the Dutch artist usually stuck to a specialty, once he had become identified with a marketable one. There were landscapists, seascapists, painters of architectural interiors, domestic interiors, animals, and a dozen others. Still-life painters had their specialties-within-a-specialty; one would become known for his ability to paint fruit; another, flowers; a third, glass and china. Willem Kalf (1622–1693) was probably the greatest of these men, a painter of strong arrangements filled with a

variety of objects in convincing relationships, as in *Still Life* (*Figure 21*).

Pieter Jansz. Saenredam (1597–1665) was one of several painters who specialized in pictures of church interiors (*Figure 22*). Unlike most of his colleagues, however, he raised these paintings above the level of perspective records and gave them a quiet, poetic character through a scheme of delicate grays, creamy and rosy tints, and accents of black with flecks of heightened color here and there in the costumes of strolling figures. Among seascapists, Willem van de Velde the Younger (1633–1707) learned his father's precise, craftsmanlike technique but elevated his art above the rank and file of seascape painting by a degree of response to the moods of nature (*Figure 23*).

But it was a landscapist, Jacob van Ruisdael (1628/29–1682), who revealed nature in the widest range of moods. Apparently he combined his career as a prolific painter with another as a physician, for he was so registered in Amsterdam. Ruisdael began as a "portrait painter" of landscape, content to reproduce familiar scenes in exact detail. But he seemed to discover nature by painting it, for he became increasingly interested in its moody variety. Sometimes he painted serenely ordered scenes, like his *Wheatfields* (Portfolio 6, Plate 66). At others he painted a storm-threatened

Figure 23

25

world of sweeping clouds, crooked trees, irregular masses of dunes, ruined buildings, and restless water. His *Cemetery* (Plate F 8) is a wonderfully romantic picture with a spectrally illuminated tomb and crumbling towers, its darkened confusion played against masses of clouds onto which the light of a clearing sky begins to pour.

Such dramatics were, generally speaking, less to the taste of the picture-buying burghers than familiar scenes from daily life, sometimes incorporating an anecdotal element. Adriaen Brouwer (1605–1638), who was born in Flanders, led a life as disorderly as the roistering scenes he painted, if we can believe the stories about him. His subject matter, usually having to do with squalor and debauchery, was not entirely new to painting, since Bruegel had previously observed peasants' carousing. But Brouwer gave it a different emphasis, deliberately setting out to be a little shocking. His art is saved from mere sensationalism or picturesque illustration by his acute study of facial expression, the fluidity of his painting, and his interest in re-creating atmospheric effects (*Figure 24*).

In the field of more conventional subject matter, two of the "Little Dutchmen," Pieter de Hooch (1629–after 1684) and Gerard Terborch (1617–1681), were successful with genre scenes of domestic life, the former being at his best when he dealt with the daily occupations of housewives, as in *Interior* (*Figure 25*); the latter in rendering satins and depicting ladies and gentlemen in equally quiet but more elegant pursuits. The apparent casualness of their subject matter can be deceptive; De Hooch, especially, was more than a "little" master in the way he painted the warm flow of light into an interior and, above all, in the way he capitalized on his unpretentious material to establish interesting space relationships between the rooms he painted and the people and the objects disposed within them. And Terborch's interest in light and texture makes him something of a small, more precise Velazquez.

He in fact observed Velazquez's work on a visit to Spain and was thereafter specifically influenced by him.

But the painter who consummated the potential of these excellent men to become, with Rembrandt, the great Dutch master of the century was Jan Vermeer of Delft (1632–1675). We have analyzed in some detail one of his most complicated pictures, *The Artist in His Studio* (Portfolio 4, Plate 37), as an arrangement of forms in space. In smaller pictures and those whose subjects offer fewer elements to be composed, Vermeer's perfection is even more impressive since it is achieved with more limited material. His *Girl Asleep* (Plate F 9) gives us the same feeling of absolute order as *The Artist in His Studio*. It is an order created without dependence on echoes of classical forms or any reference to the theories of classical art, yet Vermeer is by the most significant definition a classical artist. Colors, textures, solid objects, the space around them, the very surface of the paint itself—everything, in short—reaches the perfect harmony,

Figure 24

26

completeness, and timelessness of true classical art, even though Vermeer paints ordinary people and simple interiors.

France and the Academy

We have seen some aspects of the art of the seventeenth century, ranging from the philosophical introspection of Rembrandt to the cool objective classicism of Vermeer, from the theatrical turbulence of *The Glorification of the Company of Jesus* to the intimate everydayness of De Hooch's *Interior*. But except for the special case of La Tour, we have said nothing about France.

We will be more occupied with the art of France than that of any other country from now on and to understand some of the conflicts that will arise we must see how, in the second half of the seventeenth century, French art took on its character as part of the fabric of the official world.

Louis XIV was king of a country at its apogee as a world power. His minister of finance, Colbert, saw the arts as an instrument of national policy, observing that the monuments created by a regime were the yardstick by which posterity measured it—as well as being impressive symbols of power in their own time. The famous portrait *Louis XIV* (Plate F10) by Hyacinthe Rigaud (1659–1743) summarizes much of the pomp, and some of the pompousness, of Louis XIV's regime as it was reflected in the art cultivated by official patronage. The old king is flatteringly represented with the beautiful legs of a ballet dancer and surrounded by billowing robes of ermine and brocade, symbols of stately power. It takes a moment to discover the face in a portrait that, in lesser hands than Rigaud's, could have been that of a royal manikin swamped by a still life of fine stuffs. But, once discovered, the face dominates the surrounding paraphernalia, revealing the old man in all his shrewdness, arrogance, and the unfaltering conviction of his own infallability that led him to characterize

Figure 25

himself for all time in the phrase, *L'état, c'est moi* (I am the state).

Louis's totalitarian machine of state had its counterpart in the Academy, formed under Colbert to insure that the arts would reflect the regime. Official art was ruled by Colbert's chosen instrument, the painter Charles Le Brun (1619–1690), a perfect man for the job since he was a skillful organizer of pictures and entire decorative schemes and the practical details necessary for carrying them out. The palace of Versailles, for which Le Brun supervised the scheme of painting, is a summation of the baroque principle of the fusion of the arts; here architecture, painting, sculpture, and landscape are organized as interdependent parts of a totality.

The world would not have lost very much if Le Brun had never painted himself; *Alexander the Great Entering Babylon (Figure 26)*, where he is at his best, is a not very imaginative demonstration showing his control of the rules of picturemaking. But in establishing these rules as dogma, he had great historical importance, as we will be seeing later.

Eventually the Academy became a hotbed of favoritism and prejudice. From the beginning Le Brun supported a group of painters called the Poussinists against their adversaries, the Rubensians. The Rubensians favored the vigorous technique, the surging composition, and particularly the warm color of the Flemish master; the Poussinists opposed to these the smoother surface, the quieter composition, and the cooler tints of Poussin.

Nicolas Poussin (1594–1665) has figured prominently in previous discussions, especially in connection with his classical landscape, *The Funeral of Phocion* (Portfolio 7, Plate 76). His *Triumph of Neptune and Amphitrite* (Plate F 11) should be placed side by side with Rubens' *Rape of the Daughters of Leucippus* (Plate F 5) to show the divergent aspects of painting that put French artists into two camps. This *Triumph* (a glorification of the sea-god and his bride) is nominally a subject of action, as Neptune on his charging horses and Amphitrite with her attendants are borne over the waves by breezes that fill scarves and lift clouds; one can imagine how Rubens would have painted it. But Poussin's arrangement is as perfectly controlled and as static as that of the landscape in *The Funeral of Phocion*, making *The Triumph* a contemplative, human-istic picture in the tradition of the painters of the High Renaissance, including Raphael. France was not ready for Poussin's revival of a classical ideal during his lifetime. He spent his most productive years in self-exile in Rome, surrounded by evidences of the tradition he loved. But by the end of the century he became the god of the Academy, which was to continue to use and misuse his principles. Poussin is still today one of the potent forces in French painting; we will continue to refer to him frequently.

France becomes, at this point in our discussions, the dominant nation in painting, leading and crystallizing the movements shared also by Germany, England, and America, while Italy relinquishes its leadership. But before we enter the next century we must see *The Procession of the Ram* (Plate F 12) by the brothers Louis (about 1593–1648) and Mathieu (1607–1677) Le Nain, who, with their elder brother Antoine (about 1588–1648), painted numerous realistic pictures of peasants in the early part

Alinari

Figure 26

28

Hooch, Pieter de	HOKE, peter de
Kalf, Willem	KOLF, WIL'm, VIL'm
Lastman, Pieter	LAST man, peter
La Tour, Georges de	la toor, zhorzh de
Le Brun, Charles	le bruhn, sharl

Le Nain, Louis, Mathieu,
    Antoine
	le nan, loo ee, ma tyuh,
	    on twon

Leonardo da Vinci	lay O NAR doe da VIN chee
Leucippus	lew SIP pus
Malle Babbe	MOL leh BOB beh
Mantegna, Andrea	mon TANE ya, AN dray a
Masaccio	ma SOTCH o
Medici	MAY dee chee
Michelangelo Buonarotti	michael AN jel o bwoe na ROT tee

Murillo, Bartolomé
    Esteban
	moo REEL yo, bar toe lo MAY
	    es TAY bon

Phocion	FO shun
Piero della Francesca	PYAIR o della fran CHESS ca
Poussin, Nicolas	poo san, nicholas
Pozzo, Andrea	POT SO, AN dray a

Raphael
    (Raffaello Sanzio)
	RAF ee ul, RAFE ee ul
	    (raf fah EL lo SAN zee o)

Ribera, Jusepe	ree BAY ra, joo SEP ay, hoo SEP ay
Rigaud, Hyacinthe	ree go, ee a sant
Rubens, Peter Paul	ROO b'nz, peter paul
Ruisdael, Jakob van	RISE dale, YAH cub, jacob van
Saenredam, Pieter Jansz.	san RAY dam, peter YONS[zone]
Terborch, Gerard	ter BORK, GER art

Tintoretto
    (Jacopo Robusti)
	tin toe RET toe
	    (YAH co po ro BOOS tee)

Titian
    (Tiziano Vecellio)
	TISH'n
	    (teet SYAH no vay CHEL yo)

Velazquez, Diego Rodríguez
    de Silva y
	ve LASS kes, ve LATH keth, dee AY go
	    ro DREE ges, ro DREE geth day
	    SEEL va ee

Velde, Willem van de	VEL de, WIL'm, VIL'm van de
Vermeer, Jan	ver MARE, yon
Verschuur, Paulus	ver SKURE, paul us
Villanueva	veel ya NWAY va
Zurbarán, Francisco de	zoor bah RAHN, thoor bah RAHN, francisco, frahn THEES co day

PRONUNCIATION GUIDE

PORTFOLIO F

THE following is intended as a simple guide to the English pronunciation commonly used in art circles of some of the foreign names and terms which appear in this seminar. No attempt has been made to use a consistent phonetic system. Pronounce each syllable as though it were English. Stressed syllables are printed in small capitals. No stress is indicated for French names which are properly pronounced with equal stress on each syllable.

Amphitrite	am fit TRY tee
Bernini, Gian Lorenzo	ber NEE nee, john lo REN zo
Bologna	bo LONE ya
Brouwer, Adriaen	BROW er, ad ree ON
Campin, Robert	com pan, ro bare
Caravaggio, Michelangelo Merisi da	car a VOD jo, michael AN jel o me REE see da
Carracci, Lodovico, Agostino, Annibale	car ROT chee, lo doe VEE co, ah gose TEE no, on nee BAH lay
Cézanne, Paul	say zan, paul
Chardin, Jean Baptiste	shar dan, zhon bah teest
chiaroscuro	key AH ro SKOO ro
Colbert, Jean Baptiste	coal bare, zhon bah teest
Dürer, Albrecht	DURE er, AL brekt
Dyck, Anthony Van	DIKE, anthony van
Eyck, van	IKE, van
Fontainebleau	fon ten blow
Fourment, Hélène	foor mon, ay len
Giotto di Bondone	JOT toe dee bon DOE nay
Goes, Hugo van der	gos, HOO go VAN der
Gonzaga	gon ZAH ga
Goya, Francisco de	GOY a, francisco, frahn THEES co day
Greco, El	GRECK o, el
Guzmán, Don Caspar de, Count Duke of Olivares	goose MON, gooth MON, don casper, cahs PAR day; o lee VAR ess
Hals, Frans	hahls, frans
Holbein, Hans	HOLE bine, hans
Hondecoeter, Melchoir D'	HON de coot er, MEL key or de

CONTINUED ON OTHER SIDE

of the seventeenth century, while Poussin, in Italy, was giving another expression of the French spirit.

The Procession of the Ram shows a folk festival. We can imagine how Brouwer might have painted it, with the carousing that, no doubt, was actually a part of it. But as painted by the Le Nains, the peasants in their picturesque costumes, realistically observed and recorded, take on nearly as much dignity as the figures of Poussin. Their rags and tatters are painted with an almost Vermeerlike love of texture; their random colors are harmonized almost as judiciously. We cannot pretend that *The Procession of the Ram* has either the profound and perfect order that justifies our calling Vermeer classical or the humanistic intellectualism that is classical in Poussin. But it is true that these simple people are not regarded as buffoons nor as inconsequential but interesting parts of a social system. They are honored, affectionately, as good people close to the simple things that are noble because they are basic to human life.

As we continue to study French painting we will see that it is animated by these two ideals —a loving and respectful response to simple things, as represented here by the Le Nains, and simultaneously a passion for rule and regulation as a discipline toward intellectual order, as represented by Poussin. There are few manifestations of the French spirit in painting in which these ideals are very far beneath the surface. Both found expression, as we have just seen, in paintings that reflected the baroque world of the seventeenth century; both played their part in developments that were to introduce the world we know.

Baroque art, from the swirling complexities of Pozzo to the monumental simplicities of Poussin and the Le Nains, reflects an age of great diversity, a century in which old traditions were carried to dramatic extremes and bold investigations presaged new departures from the direction of the past.

The eighteenth century, the subject of our next discussion, is the dividing period between a world that must remain for us the distant past and a world that we think of as the immediate background of our own experience.

Color Plates

Figures in the Text

17. THE MAN WITH THE GOLDEN HELMET, about 1650, by Rembrandt Harmensz. van Ryn (1606–1669), Dutch

Oil on canvas. Height 26¾". Kaiser Friedrich Museum, Berlin

18. THE RETURN OF THE PRODIGAL SON, 1636, by Rembrandt Harmensz. van Ryn (1606–1669), Dutch

Etching. Height 6¼". The Metropolitan Museum of Art, bequest of Ida Kammerer in memory of her husband, Frederic Kammerer, M.D., 1933

19. SELF-PORTRAIT AS A YOUNG MAN, by Rembrandt Harmensz. van Ryn (1606–1669), Dutch

Oil on wood. Height 8⅝". The Metropolitan Museum of Art, bequest of Evander B. Schley, 1952

20. SELF-PORTRAIT, 1660, by Rembrandt Harmensz. van Ryn (1606–1669), Dutch

Oil on canvas. Height 31⅝". The Metropolitan Museum of Art, bequest of Benjamin Altman, 1913

21. STILL LIFE, 1659, by Willem Kalf (1622–1693), Dutch

Oil on canvas. Height 23". The Metropolitan Museum of Art, Maria DeWitt Jesup Fund, 1953

22. SAINT BAVO IN HAARLEM, by Pieter Jansz. Saenredam (1597–1665), Dutch

Oil on wood. Height 32⅝". The John G. Johnson Collection, Philadelphia

23. ENTRANCE TO A DUTCH PORT, by Willem van de Velde the Younger (1633–1707), Dutch

Oil on canvas. Height 25⅞". The Metropolitan Museum of Art, bequest of William K. Vanderbilt, 1920

24. THE SMOKERS, by Adriaen Brouwer (1605–1638), Flemish

Oil on wood. Height 18". The Metropolitan Museum of Art, the Michael Friedsam Collection, 1931

25. INTERIOR, by Pieter de Hooch (1629– after 1684), Dutch

Oil on canvas. Height 20⅝". The Toledo Museum of Art

26. ALEXANDER THE GREAT ENTERING BABYLON, by Charles Le Brun (1619–1690), French

Oil on canvas. Height 14' 9". The Louvre Museum, Paris